NATIVE AMERICANS

AZTEC

Big Buddy Books
An Imprint of Abdo Publishing
www.abdopublishing.com

Sarah Tieck

www.abdopublishing.com

Published by Abdo Publishing, a division of ABDO, PO Box 398166, Minneapolis, Minnesota 55439.
Copyright © 2015 by Abdo Consulting Group, Inc. International copyrights reserved in all countries. No part
of this book may be reproduced in any form without written permission from the publisher. Big Buddy Books™
is a trademark and logo of Abdo Publishing.

Printed in the United States of America, North Mankato, Minnesota.
102014
012015

Cover Photo: © NativeStock.com/Angel Wynn; Shutterstock.com.
Interior Photos: ASSOCIATED PRESS (p. 5); *Getty Images*: LUIS ACOSTA/Staff (p. 23), DEA PICTURE LIBRARY
    (p. 13); *Glowimages.com*: Werner Forman Archive/Museum for Volkerkunde, Basel. Location: 28 (p. 17);
    ©iStockphoto.com (pp. 21, 30); © National Geographic Image Collection/Alamy (pp. 15, 17); © NativeStock.
    com/Angel Wynn (pp. 9, 17, 29); © North Wind Picture Archives (pp. 11, 25, 27); Shutterstock.com (p. 19); ©
    Steve Vidler/Alamy (p. 16).

Coordinating Series Editor: Rochelle Baltzer
Contributing Editors: Bridget O'Brien, Marcia Zappa
Graphic Design: Adam Craven

Library of Congress Cataloging-in-Publication Data

Tieck, Sarah, 1976-
  Aztec / Sarah Tieck.
    pages cm. -- (Native Americans)
  ISBN 978-1-62403-576-0
1. Aztecs--Juvenile literature. I. Title.
  F1219.73.T525 2015
  972--dc23
                        2014028398

CONTENTS

Amazing People

Hundreds of years ago, North America was mostly wild, open land. Native Americans lived on the land. They had their own languages and **customs**.

The Aztec (AZ-tehk) are one Native American group. They are known for their powerful kings and beautiful cities. They built one of the world's greatest **civilizations**. Let's learn more about these Native Americans.

Did You Know?

The Aztecs first called themselves the *Mexica*. Later, people began calling them *Aztecs*.

Aztecs traditionally wore colorful headdresses.

Aztec Territory

Aztec homelands were in the heart of Mexico. Mexico and Central America are known as Mesoamerica. This land is covered with jungles and swamps. There are also lakes, valleys, and mountains.

AZTEC HOMELANDS

MEXICO

GUATEMALA

UNITED STATES

MEXICO

CUBA

BELIZE

GUATEMALA

HONDURAS

EL SALVADOR

NICARAGUA

COSTA RICA

PANAMA

N
W E
S

7

HOME LIFE

Many Aztec families lived in one-story homes with more than one room. The rooms faced a courtyard. There was a kitchen and a fire for cooking in the courtyard.

Farmers lived in small huts. These were covered with woven twigs and clay. Homes for the wealthy or city leaders were made from stone or **adobe**.

Today, Aztec villages are gone. People try to show what they might have looked like long ago.

What They Ate

The Aztec were skilled farmers. They planted crops on floating gardens called chinampas. Plants grew well in these gardens.

Aztecs grew beans, squash, and maize, or corn. They also grew tomatoes, potatoes, and avocados. The men fished. They hunted deer, rabbit, armadillos, and snakes. Aztecs bought or traded for food at markets, too.

Did You Know?

Many Aztec foods remain popular today. Some include chili pepper, avocado, and drinking chocolate.

Chinampas were made by digging up soil from lake bottoms.

Daily Life

At the peak of Aztec **civilization**, there were millions of Aztecs. The people lived in cities, towns, and villages. The city of Tenochtitlán (tay-nawch-teet-LAHN) had about 200,000 people. It was built in Lake Texcoco on an island.

Aztec women wore wraparound skirts and sleeveless shirts. Men wore **loincloths**. They also wore cloaks that tied over one shoulder. Nobles wore clothes that were colorful and decorated.

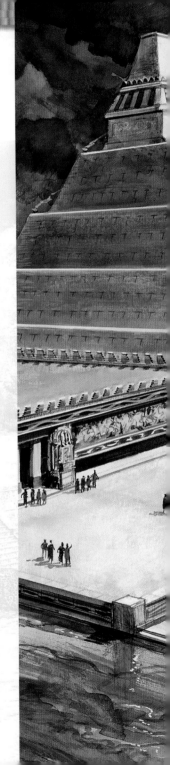

Tenochtitlán was known for its size and beauty. There were temples and pyramids.

Aztec people had different jobs. Men farmed or worked at a trade. They were warriors, builders, artists, priests, or kings. Women took care of the home. They cooked food and wove cloth. Some worked as healers.

At birth, Aztec girls got brooms or sewing baskets. Baby boys got tools or shields and arrows. Young kids had chores. When they got older, they attended boarding schools. Girls married by about age 16. Boys married around age 20.

Today, Aztec women continue traditions, such as making corn tortillas.

15

MADE BY HAND

The Aztec made many objects by hand. They often used natural materials. But many times, they used gold, silver, or jewels. These arts and crafts added beauty to everyday life.

Mosaic

The Aztec decorated sculptures with mosaics. These were made by arranging materials, including shells and turquoise, into a pattern.

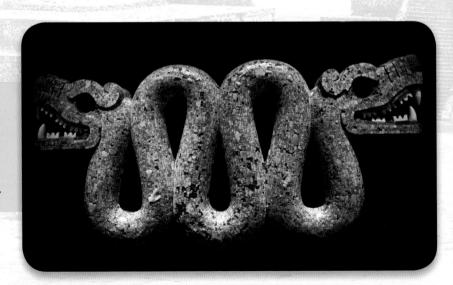

Jewelry
The Aztec made jewelry from feathers, precious stones, gold, and silver. Most jewelry was owned or traded by wealthy Aztecs.

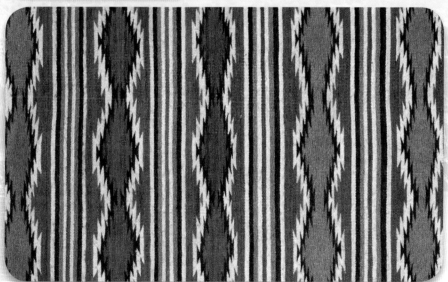

Stone Sculptures
Aztecs carved objects from different types of stone. They used volcanic rock and jade. Some works were small. Others were more than ten feet (3 m) tall.

Woven Cloth
Aztec women were skilled weavers. They spun fibers into yarn, and then wove yarn into cloth. People often dyed their clothing different colors. Wealthy people could afford to wear brighter clothes.

Spirit Life

Aztec religion was based on nature. The people honored several gods. *Huitzilopochtli* (hweets-ee-loh-PAWCH-tlee) was the god of war. *Quetzalcóatl* (kweht-suhl-kuh-WAH-tuhl) was the god of learning.

The Aztec honored their gods with **ceremonies** and **rituals**. Sometimes, they **sacrificed** humans for their gods. They believed this helped their kings, cities, and people stay healthy and prosper.

The ancient city of Teotihuacán (tay-oh-tee-wah-KAHN) was an important religious site for the Aztecs. They believed the gods created the world there.

STORYTELLERS

The Aztec used stories and art to teach people their history and religion. Some stories were about how their people fit into the world.

The legend of the Fifth Sun describes five worlds. The Aztecs live in the world of the Fifth Sun, which is ruled by the sun god *Tonatiuh*. The story says the people must honor this god with blood **sacrifices** or their world would be destroyed.

The Aztec Calendar Stone has images of the legend of the Fifth Sun carved into it.

A Strong Civilization

Aztecs are believed to have come from the north around 1200. In about 1325, the tribe founded its capital Tenochtitlán. It became one of the world's largest cities.

At first, the Aztec were ruled by a chief. Later, they had a king. Eventually, the Aztec were ruled by an emperor. This person was known as the Great Speaker.

The Aztec were fierce fighters. They took over other tribes. Their **civilization** was one of the most powerful of its time.

Did You Know?

In about 1375, Acamapichtli became the first Aztec king.

Today, people act out what Aztec daily life was like in the past.

In 1519, Hernán Cortés and Spanish **conquistadors** arrived in Tenochtitlán. Aztec emperor Montezuma II welcomed them. But, the Spanish wanted to control the great city. They captured Montezuma II and he died. By 1521, the people and their city fell.

Cortés took over and built what is now Mexico City. Many Aztecs died from Spanish diseases. By 1700, much of Aztec **culture** had faded. Today, **descendants** of the Aztecs live in Mexico.

Did You Know?

Montezuma II ruled more than 5 million people.

Many historians believe Montezuma II and the Aztecs thought Cortés was their god Quetzalcóatl. They had long told stories about the return of this god with light skin.

Back in Time

1428

The Aztec cities of Tenochtitlán, Texcoco, and Tlacopán formed an alliance. This allowed them to grow strong and powerful.

About 1325

The Aztec founded Tenochtitlán.

1440

Montezuma I became the Aztec ruler. He was a strong fighter. He is considered the father of the Aztec empire.

About 1200

The Aztec came from the north. They were farmers who moved often.

1519

Hernán Cortés, of Spain, arrived on Aztec land. The Aztec welcomed him and his people.

1521

Cortés and the Spanish took over Tenochtitlán after a battle. More than 200,000 people died. The Spanish destroyed the city and began building what is now Mexico City.

THE AZTEC TODAY

The Aztec people have a long, rich history. They are remembered for their powerful kings, beautiful cities, and successful farming methods.

Aztec roots run deep. Even though times have changed, many people carry the **traditions**, stories, and memories of the past into the present.

Did You Know?

Today, many Native Americans living in and around Mexico City are Aztec descendants.

Aztec families prepare for a dance by donning traditional clothing and headdresses.

"I confide to your care my beloved children, the most precious jewels I can leave you. The great monarch beyond the ocean will interest himself to see that they come into their inheritance, if you present before him their just claims. I know your master will do this, if for no other reason, then for kindness I have shown the Spaniards . . ."

— The last words of Montezuma II to Hernán Cortés

GLOSSARY

adobe (uh-DOH-bee) a type of brick or building material made from sun-dried earth and straw.

ceremony a formal event on a special occasion.

civilization a well-organized and advanced society.

conquistador (kahn-KEES-tuh-dawr) a leader in the 1500s Spanish conquests of America, Mexico, and Peru.

culture (KUHL-chuhr) the arts, beliefs, and ways of life of a group of people.

custom a practice that has been around a long time and is common to a group or a place.

descendant (dih-SEHN-duhnt) a member of the same family.

loincloth a simple cloth worn by a man to cover his lower body.

ritual (RIH-chuh-wuhl) a formal act or set of acts that is repeated.

sacrifice a person or animal killed as an offering to please a god.

tradition (truh-DIH-shuhn) a belief, a custom, or a story handed down from older people to younger people.

WEBSITES

To learn more about Native Americans, visit **booklinks.abdopublishing.com**. These links are routinely monitored and updated to provide the most current information available.

INDEX